AMERICAN FALL
POEMS

ACKNOWLEDGEMENTS

I must acknowledge the enormous contributions to this volume made by Wayne Brown and Derek Walcott, who both gave me scholarships to their workshops, and were kind enough to look at my work long after the workshops ended. The Trinidad Theatre Workshop and the Beryl McBurnie Foundation of Trinidad also provided financial assistance toward attending Mr Walcott's workshop at Boston University in the Fall of 2000.

AMERICAN FALL
POEMS

RAYMOND RAMCHARITAR

PEEPAL TREE

First published in Great Britain in 2007
Peepal Tree Press Ltd
17 King's Avenue
Leeds LS6 1QS
UK

ISBN 13: 978 1 84523 043 2

Peepal Tree gratefully acknowledges Arts Council support

CONTENTS

For my wife, Adele,
without whom there would be no poetry

AMERICAN FALL

I
America's fall is her most perfect
season – not for the early twilights,
storms and gray days – though the night's
changing brings its own magic –
but the smaller moments it opens –
instants where the eye and rivers
cross, leaving clarity, as the punts' slivers
slice the Charles toward the ends
of the cool Boston evenings. Watching
it all along the pitched bank path –
the thudding runners' hearts, the start
of dusk's theatre – there is so much in
these things for the outsider: the wondrous
civic sureness of the behemoth
trams constrained in their tracks; the argot,
loud and public, but always conscious
of purity; the native tenseness
of guarding the scheme of America –
its rise, its fall, its coming winter –
certain of the evening solstices
that plane wildness into cities,
whose untidy trees and steel
gauze window frames retain the feel
of places and seasons kept from me.

II
September, when the leaves begin
their dying spirals, Boston sits
alert in the weakening light, its
avenues alive with the faces, the din
of the Fall's colours, dialects
that drown mine; colours – saffrons, blues –

bodies and landscape fusing – hues of
a multifoliate dialectic
I cannot penetrate – a dreary
story: alone in a cool city,
seeing it passionately, with the
outsider's desire for sanctuary
among the amnesiac boulevards
or the bland, moss-covered houses.
The unreasoning sadness it rouses
looks away from the centre, towards
home: shards of a city much like Dis –
as distant from cool gray evenings
as the Charles' glassy face from the heavings
of the passionate Atlantic we cross.

III

Outside the windows of my room
one tree flowered through November;
its slow death a song that remembered
my passage, its body a yellow plume
pointing to the tainted house
that harboured me, as the other trees,
registering the native unease,
looked down from their in-furled boughs –
the world behind the warm facades
of smiles and promises no one
is bound by – grand ideas broken
by a coloured America, its guards
confused, its premises reversed
by this new definition of freedom
that takes America from them,
eliciting a ruthless commerce
with the East, South, the underworld
of those unfinished cities – the hells
that consume the dreams she expels –

taking pixels for food and gold
to provide each desperate body with
an allotment of non-redeemable hope,
like the lone flowering tree in the zoetrope
of a Fall whose reach is infinite.

TWO POEMS ON THE DEATH OF A CHILD

I

The first week, your mother cried every day;
your father a little braver.
I could only hide in the silence in between,
speaking in forlorn moments
of the beauty of little things
amidst the plainness loss brings.

And if a final cigarette is offered
to grieving, dying men,
I would beg the script finished, the director
awoken, actors found;
and then I could bow, having seen
footprints where emptiness had been.

II

Your mother sits alone.
Solemnity sits like an owl
on the house. The children play
too quietly. The dog does not howl.

My brother, the children, the dog
in their places. I sit like fate,
as an eye raises, searches,
then descends slowly, to wait.

Some evenings in St. Ann's, the tall hedges
around the house trap the light, uncurling
the body's spiral to night-time places.
                              And I know,
undoubtedly, this thing we've made is dying.

Now like night, the time of dark suits
approaches. The days spread out
beyond the moment. The closed room
is readied to receive the honoured guest.

I will not observe the seven days'
mourning; nor the forty days' pieties;
nor the feast at the end of the year. Except
my regret, nothing is sacred here.

TRAIN TRACKS

Something poetic there is about train tracks.

Something about the patience in the steady
parallelism of the ablated shale and gravel lying
along the theoretical space between the tracks.

Something sad, like the existential green weed
defying the winter to challenge the greyness
between the out-flung stations of the world.

Something joyous about the sudden
curves away from the endless straightness; the junction
boxes sentrying the spaces between towns.

Something huge and furious there is
that rages through the untiring trains
and the souls racing toward their final end.

THE PRISONER

Dinner: a ritual of careful placement:
the careful food on the silver platter;
the careful display of his best manner.
But through the careful, anguished chatter,
the gleaming knives, the polished stems
of aloof glasses, the gleaming smiles,
outside the empty house, the galleon
of the Moon sails over his careful wiles.

CENTAUR

And I saw a new heaven and a new earth: for the first
heaven and the first earth were passed away

Revelations, 21:1

I

"No sun, no rain, nothing; everything fine."
He grins in the darkness. Tiresias: he would
have forgotten more ghosts than I will ever know.
("I remember when we used to fight for food.")

Now night undoes the order of the new
Aegean. The tribes – the slaves of Ashanti and Xhosa,
the scions of waylaid Brahmins and pariahs –
all seek in the sleep of warm amnesia

their pure origins, making wasted lands
of these jewelled paths left by Socrates,
our true Redeemer. Centaurs, between worlds,
searching Malbolges: ruins which were never cities.

II

We who are powerless, all power seeks to
conquer. With the hooves of stallions, we tread
through the sky-roofed halls, over roots that grow
into the brimming earth, feeding off the dead

and the living. We must write these songs.
Who else will notice when the sparrow falls?
Who else will chronicle the crying seas?
Between the races, who will jump the walls?

Now, the wall cuts deep into dead earth, and
night palls the distant voices of aging gods.
We are the new gods, we who woke without
memory, to the songs of clashing swords.

MUSEUM PIECE

I

I remember a time when your mother
looked as you look – only in different
light – she beside the props of a mythy
scene of the early impressionists, cajoling
reticent Corot: "The nose, you must
make it straighter, dear Camille, like a
cameo Victorian women wore…"

II

You have entered places your mother's
words and their distant echoes could not –
dark-lit places, amidst rough men,
nervily gauging their rough intent.
(Strange those moments. The weaker light
reveals in chiaroscuro what the sun,
source of dappled light that haloes her,
scarce suspects: the essentialness of
final moments – after raging against its
foreseen, but still shocking emptying.)

III

Emptying gives certainty. Your real
end dispenses salvation, not triumphal
rebirth. Here, reality follows the light;
flickers, flutters; strobes of sublimated
terrors of the deep against the walls.
The newfangled magic that follows finds
organza transparencies: a childhood
you cannot escape in daylight.
Something grander must turn these
songs inward to serener illusions.)

IV

Mornings – early dawn – light the only
room unreal enough to house such longing.
Haloed, back-lit, regally arrayed, she awaits
your steps trapping up the stairs –
luminescent from the men's endearments –
like Penelope, wifely, contemptuous virtue
confronting you finally, seeking revenge
after their defeat and hers, revenge for
womanhood your unfolding eclipsed.

LOVE STORY

I

Two years they lived alone up there, with trees
and birds for neighbours, envying the mountains'
relentless strength. The mornings were best for his pains
which lifted up to meet the sun, but which night seized
back to earth; so night was her time to heal him
with news she brought of the pale living world
he'd enraged to eruption, which had hurled
his life into her patient arms. The dim
light he brought to her in his eyes had grown,
she saw, watching the line of a brown finger
tracing his black-flecked profile, bringing her
into the fantasy of gowns she had sewn
awaiting princes on white chargers. But he
was no prince – nor anything so noble or whole
as a dream – just a man weakness would hold
from flight, and freedom was all he could see.

II

The mountains' colours mimed their lives: the green –
their high country escaped the yearly Fall – and
the gray – that every landscape harbours. In sand
or rocks or forests, even the grandest skein
of nature retains a living memory
of original tragedy. In the world
before theirs, he'd been a poet, but doled
a life from the newspapers. A story,
carelessly told, had caused a death. His life
in a fool's payment gave its fire to gray.
She'd flickered on the edge of his life that day
she saw the turning: the corners led to strife
away from hope. She pitied the bowed head
and took him in as sacrifice, to recall
the words she'd never dared to speak, for all
his life, in sacrifice for the world's quiet, had dared.

III

She thought of him as her beautiful captive
and, early on, left him with pens and paper
saying: "Write it all down, release the vapour
of death; you're alive, you have no choice but to live –
then write me a love story." The rest she left
to solitude and the mountains, as she descended
into the city each day. The story's end did
not occur to her, because the cleft
between the real and fiction had disappeared
for them, healed with the human follies
the first pair had bequeathed with their fall. His
uniting the halves which artifice had paired
had, she thought, rediscovered something
she'd a memory of, but no living sense.
But he'd been taught by his experience:
Illusion was hell's most deceptive ring.

IV

The story he'd begun to write was ending
and so, he knew, was the life he shared with her.
He thought of her as nurse, his muse and lover,
but now, he expected death – had seen the blending
of life and its opposite too early. Now,
too soon aware of transience, without
the graces of youth and vanity, his mouth
had lost the sweetness of life, nothing could grow
inside him; he felt his body a wretched anchor
holding him fast, and dreamed only of release.
He saw life as an animal that would only cease
when his eyes closed. He thought to thank her
before he left; the story he composed
was a long blessing to her. It closed saying:
"Do you know, all this time I have been praying
you would see what's here is not man, but ghost."

RHYMING DANTE

(for winston bailey)

The songs created from sounds never sung
by any single voice: the sounds choral;
the chorus of a race: but which? No race
contains the blackness they brought the world, the umbral

blackness of ideas or evil, or the purest
idea of evil; and complete, as Dante
tapered his gyres (and more complete, for Beatrice
waited below, and when hell finds entente

with hope, fear leaves the world, and world becomes
a place of echoes of light striking empty
vessels.) These songs which map the lengths of souls;
songs of the damned few amidst the plenty,

the songs we would never understand, or their
conscription of the things we felt we knew
into armies we could not see, and which
even if we could see, would not want to.

STATE OF GRACE

I
Ephemera of the morning: the drained cup,
the muted cards on the cushion covering
her knees, the alert eyes mirroring the
dying etheric fire.
            He is lulled by
the coffee, cigarettes, considerations
of shimmering mythic possibilities –
moon-marked paths on water.
                He considers
a future mapped by cards – the alluring map
the aging voice describes seems somehow clearer

than the science of maps he knows: the fate
he follows is blind and he rejoices at her
sublime sureness over unimagined ground.
And though he knows the words, he listens still.
The ritual is all, and the admonitions,
precise as litany, sooth like childhood prayers.
She leads him gently with her voice, and watches
him dissolve into the newly-wrought world.

II
"Listen," she says, "to this story – about a girl."

Ah, Gracie, he thinks, what huger life could you
create? What place is more magnificent
than the countries you conceive from the dead cards?

"A country girl, she is young, beautiful.
But her father, he is cruel, cruel to her,
but then, at sixteen, someone takes her away."
I see travel, and then fulfilment comes.
You will meet a man who will help you. Patience.

A stranger will come into your life: a woman
older than you — see here? the Queen of Swords
I see a romance.

              "But he is a good man;
and when he takes her, takes her gently. She comes
to love him."

            I can see your life, Gracie,
the life you search these cards to find, the life
you call us here to witness. The good man:
the father, the husband you left in the dead of night?

"The man is a good man. He is alone,
he marries her, and makes her his partner, sends
her to the best schools — Paris, Switzerland.
She becomes a lady..."

              A dark woman,
an unexpected situation; beware
betrayal.

      "Years pass and she remembers
the old place, the old life (Oh, I will give
her adventures in the mean). And then, one day
she returns."

          The Wheel of Fortune is also
the wheel of fate. Each is bound to his fate,
none can escape — remember, nothing is left to
chance, all that exists serves the divine plan.

"She goes to the old man, the father, to spit
on him. But when she sees him so old, weak,
she realises all is as all should be.
Her life was not an accident. She leaves.
The end."

III

He visits her sometimes on dreary, hopeless
mornings in the old house. She embraces
him with a strange warmth he receives with hapless
confusion, as with the otherworldly graces
she extends to him – memories of a fabulous
past she has told him of, and which, he knows,
she will tell again between the meticulous
dissections of his fate.
                              It is this that draws
him here, to the old house. He knows the world
she contrives from the cards has no existence
in any place except in the cool, bold
excursions of her voice across the distance
that separates them. He knows of her life
here amidst the ghosts:
                              she is an old woman
in an old house: he feels the marks of strife
in the wavering uncertainty of her hand
as it touches his hand.
                              He considers this as she reads
the signs of favoured fortune and the will
of God, waiting for her to tire of deeds
undone, and even unconsidered, until
the cards themselves tire and describe airy
improbabilities. Her hands become
tired as the cards become tired and quietly
she softens the clamour of morning to a hum.
She arranges the sounds into a stately
procession of memories, and makes a song
remembering evenings in a bright city.
He imagines a time when the world was young,
when even the life of the new world unfurled
at her command, and in the evenings
of a cool summer that only she could end,
she became the shining centre of all things.

He is silent as he watches her life spend
itself visiting imagined kingdoms.
He thinks: As well for this as any death,
for death is the same dreary carriage that comes
and life is just a gorgeous device to forget.

IV
He leaves the haloed house thinking of death
and forever. The place she brings him to is new,
somehow. Always the images that arise
seem to remember a stranger architecture
than any he can create in his fictions.
The road leading him away, to his old life,
seems somehow wider, and it is this –
the leaving – that brings him always back.
He thinks of his own house, and his own life
and the lives enacted along the road he walks.
He contemplates the opiate fictions:
the wife, the children, the white dreams
that he could touch once – the boughs were so close! –
now as estranged to him as she to her life.
A profusion of memories and impulses
follow him from the house – ideas, colours
rages of sensations, impressions so distant
he can scarce believe that he was the maker.
"How is it that I who made these things have
lost them so completely?" he asks softly,
and softer remembers they that wait on him,
they to whom his life belongs, and quickens
his steps, shrugging off nearer memories
that cling like children. Before it closes he thinks:
"Perhaps a better place awaits us somewhere.
Perhaps after the last, blinding flash
we wake in a large room, on a large bed
to anxious faces and different memories."

SETTLING IN
(for Nathan Hazel)

The night befriends the prey, and the body's
inviolable logic defeats the mind.
I know the signs. I descend from my howdah
as dusk begins to loose the threads that bind

the light to the corners in rooms of my house.
Inside, it is all as I ordained: the sheets
are starched, the door ajar, the light adjusted
to match the moon. In here, the mind retreats.

Deceiving the body with sleep, darkness dissolves
the ideas of flesh. Into this order,
and cloaked by the standards of night, I advance.
drawing the sheets aside, I close the purdah

to the houris of sleep. I know the pleasure
of remembered pleasures. But I am an old man
approaching an end. Now veils excite me more
than flesh. Now, there are no flames left to fan.

The sap of life recedes, the body slows,
the mind restores its memories and shuns
the shadows that harbour unrepentant truths.
Now, the act in conception supplants actions.

Regret stalks me like a tiger. I nurtured
its cubs with fear. Now, there is no gratitude,
only justice. The skein unravels slowly:
a waltz, without music to set the mood.

ISHMAEL

You are going to have a son and you
will name him Ishmael. But your son will live
like a wild beast. He will be against every one
And everyone will be against him.
                                        Genesis 17:11

For years you waited, looking for signs, and then,
like a child, you wished it out of nothing.
Beginning, you fed it, stroked its joints with oil
to make them supple. The strength would come
as years and seasons passed, leaving their wholeness:
the completeness of a tree ascending the air:
a life artificing life. You did not
know this at the start – that in creating it, it
created you, as a child does; although
you knew it was not a child.

Still, you nurtured it, let your blood warm it;
you let your heart, in time, become its heart,
and listening to your heart, you heard its song.

It was not a child, but like a child you knew
the time was coming: limbs had begun to grow,
wings had formed, its life was slowly unfurling,
separate from you, along a path you
could not see or follow. Until you saw
the inexorable claws, and the heaviness
of its existence draw it away from you.
You watched, like Daedalus, the fragile wings
flutter, saw the hungry eyes imprison
the sunlight in its brutish memory.

And thus, when the time came,
your knowledge was useless, for although you knew
it was not a child, you gave it your heart. Your blood
was mixed with its brute's blood. And when it fell,
your blood made the sea the colour of wine.

Listen, I have tasted the sea water:
the purple echoes of rage still resound.

12.30 SHOW

The music accompanies the hero
as closely as your eyes.

The city's in danger; the woman
waits amidst a sylvan scene.

The scene is as you would have it:
the calculated imperfections

(seamless canopies of thought
covering the world —

magnificent presumptions! The lives
unknown but so precisely assumed!)

consigning fabulous determined fates
to darkened considerations.

The camera's ambit is the universe,
an eye that mimics your own unseeing life:

the darkness from which we came,
the darkness to which we return.

EPITHALAMIUM

I

The wedding on the beach, another thing
you always thought you'd do, but in the end,
I know, you saw yourself surrendering
the tie-dyed romance for the satin send-off,
crying when you should be smiling, deserting,
like album photos, joy for solemnity –
the collars and veils, grimaces portending hurt,
or as if virtue required severity.

II

You laughed in all our pictures, even though
it rained, and the priest wore a baseball cap
and married us beneath Pound's wet, black bough
on the soft sand, smiling at your burlap
veil. I loved you more for letting me
think it was your choice, despite everything –
your mother's memories, her white dress and the
moments that still glittered when she looked at her ring.

III

And then we were alone in the small house,
wondering if this was how it felt to be married –
the new geography of the bed, saying "ours"
instead of "mine" or "your parents'", and being worried
about tax credits, warranties – a gradual
descent into the world of slow decay
known as death – and then the knowledge that all
we knew and were had been before; each day
inside the little house had grown and died
before along the water-stained walls; the recurrent
roses outside had witnessed love elide
into life – then the wonder if life meant
always the end of something: youth, sweetness –
all this in the first month!

Someday, only the roses
and the house will remain, with the first happiness
between the spaces of the slowing years.

PURE SOUND

(For Ken Ramchand)

Disciples of pure sound are in their hearts
optimists: no science unhinges the ocean
they say, and autopsies its hidden parts;
they scoff at theories, relying on unseen

providence that raises oaks and mountains,
such certainty it is that drives the sun
through its days, through epochs of loss and gain,
through times of wood, then stone, then bronze and iron

then back again. Disciples of pure sound
do not consider the night in their strong songs
of praise. Even dreaming, they dance around
the entropy that seethes between rights and wrongs;

inside their hooded cloaks, they go naked
before the complex world, waxing as it wanes;
rewriting signs and reading wonders, they make
its mysteries plain, and balm its intricate pains

with salves of divine structure, smiling all the while.
Deconstructing doubt, disciples of pure sound
seem bemused at science's denial
of their magic that makes the world go round.

GREEN LIPSTICK.

(found poem)

Do you want to know what
the secret of beauty is?

Bright red lipstick leaning toward pink
is beautiful with your hair

but it clashes with your skin.
Cranberry brings out the lovely

emerald highlights in your eyes
but it makes the skin-tone look lizardy.

Scarlet is perfect for your skin,
but it makes the auburn in your hair

look like a fright wig
Your hair and skin are begging

for fuschia, but your eyes
are screaming

No! No! No!

(from an 'Ernie' comic in the *Trinidad Sunday Express*, Nov. 1997)

AFTER STEVENS

Sometimes I forgot, or it could be I let myself
forget. Even the music, not at all
funereal – never stopping or closing
itself – did not mistake the steely intent

her sureness brought with it, desiring nothing
but absolutes, the perfection of music being
among the things she chose to conscript
into her fabulous world. For it was

the way she saw the world that drew all things
to her: the strange aristocratic kindness
which revealed to everything its place in the world.
Perhaps it was not a complete perfection,

perhaps what I saw as kindness was not that:
perhaps I forgot, or, blinded by her
involuntary magic, I could do
nothing else amidst the scented enchantments

that surrounded her. Perhaps I knew
what I knew (or what I thought I knew)
only because it pleased her to show me.
Still, I understood that by her showing me,

the music would never be the same again.
Her sureness would be all that mattered to me;
I gladly deserted memories – the mere
act of memory becoming hopeless

as the whispers that trailed the dresses she wore –
for the new life the music's changing tempo
presaged. The world within a world created
outside the world. Slowly. Fading. Away.

II

Later, after searching in vain for seven
years, I closed my eyes to rest, and
sightless, could hear, suddenly, the music.
Then all at once it became clear: even

the city had known, and knowing it, had made
the roofs cymbals, and the spires flutes to welcome
your magic – which travelled through sound and not sight,
and which, in dreams I had heard, but could never persuade

my waking sight was real. (So that explained
the respectful silences as we walked the streets
and your stranger confusion at my blind anger;
and your composure – as still as the steely planed

surfaces the orchestral buildings heralded
your passing upon.) And the birds knew, and knowing
forsook their necessary journeys, unmade
their arrows and formed canopies instead,

quilts that tested the wideness of the sky's intent
against the hugeness of the song that runnelled
along the eaves and beneath and around the city
leaving the streets enchanted and the trees content.

III

In time I will remember you like this:
the eyes; the hair, let down and shiny black;
the moment's startling nakedness against
the sky requiting my surrendered bliss.

My memory will remain passionless,
architectural: a lesser beauty
preserved in the lesser kingdom of thought;
a painted image: complete, pitiless.

THE SECRET OF FLIGHT

Five miles up, the grating turbo props
rattle the fiction of familiarity
but not enough –

even from this height, the sea exhausts
the eye.

Does the eagle fear for his kingdom?

Solitary soarer, artist of clouds' brooding
morphologies –
            perilous escarpments,
nodulous spheres, pale suspended savannahs –
planes of ineffable dimensions.
                         Seeking
such ineffable height, I see Daedalus
who kept the middle course as Icarus fell.

O earthly life, O creature between fiction and real,
will you ever see such joy worth dying for?

VILLANELLE

In time the world approached its former brightness.
The sun continued to rise, the seasons resumed,
and all but me forgot the gorgeous whiteness

you showed the world, increasing its ordained light
in ways the later brightness had never presumed.
In time the world approached its former brightness

but imperfectly: seeing its former height
as early passion, irrevocably consumed;
and all but me forgot the saving whiteness

of flames that licked against the silence of night;
retreating to huge dreams as lives were entombed
in time. The world approached its former brightness –

bearing gifts in procession through the bright
cynosure where your flowers could still bloom,
and all but me forgot the gorgeous whiteness

but saw, in dreams, a body fading from sight
through the clouds with the foresight of the doomed.
In time the world approached its former brightness
and all but me forgot the saving whiteness.

DAGUERROTYPE

I
And just as promised, it was the little things
that still worked in the end. The intricate
human machinery, the heart and its countries —
the things that had learned to exist invisibly
just outside our transfixed sight
impervious to the doom-driven night.

II
I first heard her laughter on such a night
containing all directions and all things
and time, baring the very air to sight,
revealing everywhere an intricate
system of dependencies, invisibly
stitching together lives as huge as countries;

assuming the huge simplicity of countries
stripped of borders in the blind joy of night.

III
And thus, mysteriously, invisibly,
she entered, showing me and thus, all things,
the design of a new life, the intricate
arraying of each sense, the blazing sight

that coloured, intensified the former sight,
bringing into existence other countries
and other geographies, the intricate
elision of all thought into the night
and all emotions and all colours. These things
she brought to me from places invisibly

existing, and silently and invisibly
emblazoning the plainness of worldly sight
with hues of dreams.

IV

                    She said: "These things
will exist independently of the countries
we have made here, long after the night
has set, leaving only the intricate

entrails of our lives on the less intricate
substrate of the real. When we invisibly
exist in the irrevocable night
and see and feel with a wisdom beyond sight,
their machinery will continue, making countries
of our memories and recreating all things."

V

Of the many things she was, her intricate
touch it was that drew countries invisibly
nearer to sight.

VI

                  Her absence is as final as night.

AFTER WILLIAMS

It is a crushed bow:
Imagine the central knot
and the two fat
wings on either side – the
material is teardrop-edged
gold gauze; the knot is
wrapped with gold wire; egrets'
feet pattern it – it fits in the
palm – feel it there; now
crush it.

Imagine
the wings closed and bruised;
in half-light, it
looks like a remnant of some large
happiness –

These are the songs she
keeps in her music
box.

THE BALLAD OF THE BORG

The end of the sky-turned faithful: regeneration
every third cycle, enhanced organic
nurture for the pale flesh the cybernetic
cannot conquer, the hierarchies and station
each receives upon assimilation –
A brutal theology that fixes
every type to its perfect unimatrix,
black armoured, drunk on the blood of the new nation –
slaves, but never so alive till the hive's
Babel; all but for the shapeless longing
that drives flesh to life – the darkness thrives
on the body but ignores the soul's feckless
physics which resists the cube's angles, droning
songs of longing into the emptiness.

YOUNG POET

"My favourite coolie," he says, and takes my hand.
I grin despite myself; it's just his way.
The stinky jokes are for relief from the grand
monuments he makes – he's on holiday.

Between the jokes, he points the famous chin
at the Little Carib stage where some youngsters
are reading the latest masterpiece – a thing in
iambic tetrameter that their tongues resist or

have been estranged from by the newfangled
schooling. I sit and practice silence in
the old theatre, like a mouse before a dangling
tidbit – that is, if you could call succession

a biscuit. When they break, he turns and asks
me how my work is going, and nods approval
at the outline of a year of a life in tasks –
the poems, a play, the hundred rejections you've

to be made of stone to ignore – "But you know
how hard it is…so…could you give me a quote?"
And there it is, I've said it, like an arrow
into the famous hazel eyes; it floats

a second, then, "I don't give blurbs. Sorry.
I know it's hard, but…" then the hot actress
enters, and the play resumes. As I hurry
to gather my things to exit, he stops and says,

"But wait awhile, we'll have a drink after."
I kind of drift to the dark seats as he
turns to the stage – the youth and laughter
of the actors, and chicks answering to honey

and darling – thinking of my deflating future;
thirty-four and still waiting for the call, as I
watch the kids wrestle iambs for an hour
sweating under the lights of his ruthless eyes.

And when they leave, we stay behind awhile
as he gathers himself – scripts in the rich black
leather bag, gold rimmed glasses, the half smile
of satisfaction as we walk onto the cracked

Woodbrook sidewalk, him beaming at the postcard
sky as I sigh at the stench of coming failure.
"But look," he says, "I'll think about that foreword
for you. I know what it's like trying from here."

My thirst evaporates after that
and I hustle to get away – why stick
around, risking caprice, when you've got what
you came for? But he can't resist a lick

in parting: "You Indians and your ambition. Black
people know how to relax, look at me."
I stare across the street as the face cracks
into another evil grin and it hits me:

It's how red niggers show coolies love – in disguise,
like saints or avatars with ancient eyes.
If he hadn't got the Nobel Prize
I'd nominate him to be canonized.

HISTORY

Somewhere along this road, it all
happened: between ancient figurations
of desire, memory and ruins ephemeral
as air, each thing awaits its epoch.

So what matters is not the real, it is the other
places that follow. Look long enough,
another city shows itself in ever
stranger ways: the voluptuous draping
of white fabric on mythic limbs; subtle
emissaries treading the borders
of the real, speaking beguiling dialects,
bringing the stranger light of another life
of larger intent, affecting visions of rapture:
golden transport to the promised place:

Here is fulfilment of ancient promises
Here is the end of endless waiting
Here is finality after the fragile mortality
vested in sullen generations
wandering through the beige-skinned deserts
following the world through its ages.

The end of such desertion is rage,
regimes of fear and uncertainty,
new theologies springing from old longing.

In rage they have painted their cages,
made of scars marks of beauty, and hunger
into music and misery into religion –
celebrating the smallness of the real.

But the cities await the instants before sleep:
moments of mystical clarity hardening

43

the unseen into sight; then trumpets will sound,
bringing to all the final dominion:

Another life, a separate place: the ships
that roll impatiently, waiting in the harbour.

ANOMIE

The impossible reduces itself to love
and physics.
        So, how – without turning eyes
to heaven, hawking the exhausted dove,
or recourse to velvety moans and purple cries –

am I to approach you? And then there's the world
whose new nature outdoes my rhetoric;
I know inside the heart of matter whirl
other worlds, but the rhythms, so small and quick,

confound my old instruments – as you do
sometimes. So if my rose-petal bedspread
is archaic, and my Romantic theories untrue,
and chaos rules our modern fragment (I've read),

we must conclude that love, like physics,
relies on perpetual motion;
               & my bags are packed
my dear, and I've thrown out all my old tricks.
Now there's the road, no map, no turning back.

CARNIVAL

Against all sense and better judgment, I'll do it
again this year, as always, because I'm trapped here;
walk out on Tuesday, down streets brimming with shit –

glass splinters, neon rags, the odd headbit –
detritus of cheap, pastiche lives – and where,
against all sense and better judgment, I do it,

snarl at the lusty anthropologists
and paradise-seeking tourists whose leers
stalk out on Tuesday, down streets brimming with shit,

cameras seizing grinning natives armed with
long spears, and decked in beads and feathers – fearless
against all sense and better judgment. I do it

every year, this useless railing against it:
the waste of songs and rage and costumes we wear,
walking out on Tuesday, down streets brimming with shit,

in a new world and time that laugh at it –
at our helping the waste of ourselves like unseen flares,
against all sense and better judgment we do it
on Carnival Tuesday, down streets brimming with shit.

RAIN SUITE
(For Steve Ouditt)

The Beetham.

Slowly, then building orchestrally, the rain thickens
like waves on the windshields, bending the wipers
with heavy washes that roll out of the stricken
sky, beating the stunned cars to a crawl along
The Beetham, whose misery persists in the new landscape –
rust, rot, blots of shacks, human absence ripe as
late Eden's white-textured descending clouds
that banish the lewd tropic detail, while outside,
the atmosphere seems to be congealing
the quiet air between the earth and its ceiling.
And the drivers, silent in their cars, remember
their first symphonies, before the resilient
self-preserving body considered, then enshrouded
the surreal "I" whose domains are the fragmented
Real. Somewhere in this erasure is escape –
the moment where each eye, encasing a different
horizon, sees the omniscient gray, perhaps;
or the water filling the spaces between craggy
dialects – or perhaps only such outpourings render
hopelesss old geographies, old sacred maps.

101: An Art Gallery

Elsewhere on this Saturday morning the rains
have flushed the city's sewers; along lanes
in Belmont, the hills' brown effluvium
repaints the whitewashed walls to the rapid drum
of martial music on the galvanized roofs.
But in St. Clair, they know how to deal with brutes –
Niggers, unions, and the weather – and here
the rain is just backdrop, steaming the bare

street, its spatter barely piercing the glazed glass
of the art gallery where they've gathered to pass
the morning lapping at wine and squinting at prints
of Pizarro's paradise, of unblemished slave skins,
And thick-limbed women in sarongs painted with flowers
with humming birds stuck in mid-pose for hours,
stunned by the emptiness of the unframed scenes –
the Canadian ambassador's wife – a green-
toothed bitch with coarse-grained skin – talking
to a Syrian cow with doughy dugs, eyes stalking
the piggy toddlers that overrun the place,
rehearsing the future, as their mother's face
dissolves gratefully in the pink two-percent
whose numbers the Pope and local business want
increased; while outside, in the dark morning,
in Laventille twenty pickneys are born
with numbers on their foreheads the rain will never
erase, although the world will try forever.

The Lookout
The slate-coloured sea that washes Port of Spain
recalls the rains sometimes into vortices
that skim along its glazed face as the city's
life reclaims the amnesia of the mundane.
You can see from the Lady Young lookout
the gray funnels stretched like thought between
the sea and sky, oblivious to the unseen
body of the land. And here, a small doubt
quavers; questioning the mind's relentless
need for prosodic regularity,
its struggle with the destiny of caprice
of nature's stubborn singularities –
the storms, volcanoes, blind tectonic shifts –
lulled by the aubade of the epoch's ingress.

Caroni

On these ululating plains, the rain is fate,
draining the Indian's ashes from the lips
of the patient Caroni, to incarnate
into the canestalks' tasselled, sky-turned tips –
arrows to the India of the mind.
While below, in patchworks of glistening strips
of razor grass and dirt, board houses on stilts
enclose the brown, work-knotted bodies,
still-sitting, folded at the hip and knee
as primal eyes grope along the endless chains
of the rain seeking escape, samadhi,
inside the dank Chaguanas cinema
where the pink, rose-lipped maidens pout and dance
in streams and around trees – a panorama
of sublimated lust, which spreads outward
through the roads outside the towns, the chance
settlements along old sugar cart-routes
where, now and then, resilient mud-spattered shards
of humanity still walk through the downpours,
of fingers which reach under rough cotton –
like the coolie farmer's trembling hand explores
his daughter's taut, brown flesh to the strum
of small bullets on the raw galvanise – to come,
hesitantly, to a stop, as the final memory
of the mother dissolves under the glare
of the unforgiving sun whose gaze clears
ruthlessly the dewy fields and glassy paths,
silencing the rain's many-armed history.

SKIMMING

The room became huge suddenly: the ceiling
expanded, curved itself to shape the sky;
the light flared, then softened into feeling.
We drifted outward, past the ploys I
brought to your voluptuous attention.

Ignored, the physics rebelled, until
finally, the elate spatial tension
collapsed, leaving a trembling truth. But still
we travelled through the constellations' pages:
the eagle, bear, the golden ass, the mule
ploughing a sensual path through the stages
of age and youth and entered the whirlpool.

Then everything stopped and there was only your voice.

You said "Ask".
                        Astonished at your directness

I faltered, fumbled around, reached for talk
of you and I, seeking relief from the awesome
gravity of our flight; and finding nothing
I sighed and asked my overwhelming question

(Leviathan, startled at my temerity,
stirred, and blinked a cloudy eye).

The moment lost its humour briefly, and quickly
regained it. Then, before the doubt could flower,
the room reclaimed its dimensions. The sky
remained round, the ceiling square, and time linear
and the world did not disturb the universe for a moment.

THE ISLAND

As he rose and fell
He passed the stages of his age and youth
Entering the whirlpool.
Gentile or Jew
O you who turn the wheel and look to windward,
Consider Phlebas, who was once handsome and tall as you.

Around the curve of the road. Dusk: a quietening. You are stretched out
along the back seat, looking at the sea that never tires.
A small island. A diagram in the sand. He was old then, an old man
beyond his years. He would have been as old then as you are now, but
already stumbling beneath the burdens of the wife, the children: burdens
you cannot conceive now.
The diagram in the sand: a point surrounded by two halves of a circle:
"This is the sea, and this is a little piece of land in the middle of it. The
sea has times when it is low and times when it is high. When it is high it
covers the island, when it is low, the island comes up."
I do not know if this is what he said: I am speaking from memory, the
memory of childhood, and it is subject to many things: rules and impres-
sions and osmosis from other memories later and stronger.
The sea has times when it is low and times when it is high. What does
this mean in the way everything we remember explains our life? And if
this is all that I remember of him, then, for me, this is the summation of
his life. All I have to remember him by. I cannot help but remember
him; there are photographs of him, a child holding a baby. The image is
indescribably sad. The baby is me.
Another memory of him: a young man in an old photograph: the beauty
of Alcibiades, sadness of a great weight already curled into the edge of
his smile, and only sadness. And this is all I knew of his life.
He was dead by the time he was my age, and buried five years later. The
drink, the children, the wife, the absolute absence of happiness.
The sea has times when it is low and times when it is high. The sea has
times when it is low and times when it is high. The two halves surround-
ing a point. Halves of a fruit? An orbit sundered? An Archimedean life,

struck down by a barbarian sword while contemplating geometry scribbled on sand? What does this mean? Who decides?

The car rounds the curve, and the sea disappears from view. The road, like the ghost's timetables, is fixed and unyielding. Now the sadness, the memories, everything, fades. You cannot possibly understand.

ACADEMIC DISCOURSE AT MIAMI

I
Miami is the perfect cure
for abstraction; as the plane touches
her skin, the speed unsheathes
the dreamy solemnity
of flight, enflaming
a lust that can take hold of nothing.

II
A city unknown to itself; the verdure
is mutinous, the identity patched
from other nations, the streets
are wide and strangely empty –
bodiless names
but for blood and pain, heeding nothing.

III
I passed through quickly, flying further
North overland, across stretches
of tamed wildness, to the neat
outline of the new city
my ticket was aimed
at, echoing the memory of nothing.

IV
The conference was a Third World affair –
twenty underfunded souls scrunched
into a cell to bleat
about art as the university
bemusedly hummed;
reminding us that it all meant nothing.

V

I escaped early; my deliverer
a young intern. As our car pushed
the interstate night, the sleek
outside dark ogled her beauty –
America's game
with her dark skin whose end is nothing.

VI

The intransit lounge is a neuter
State where the images and flush
of smallness and effete
cant diffuse reality
into a frame
seeking in air the solace of nothing.

VII

And here, in the air, only water
means what it means below – so much is
evident; it completes
nothing; the only quality
it cares to claim
is absence: a nature needing nothing.

ALSO NEW FROM TRINIDAD

Jennifer Rahim
Songster and Other Stories
ISBN: 9781845320487; pp. 146; £7.99; published July 2007

Rahim's stories move between the present and the past to make sense of the tensions between image and reality in contemporary Trinidad. The contemporary stories show the traditional, communal world in retreat before the forces of local and global capitalism. A popular local fisherman is gunned down when he challenges the closure of the beach for a private club catering to white visitors and the new elite; the internet becomes a rare safe place for an AIDS sufferer to articulate her pain; cocaine has become the scourge even of the rural communities. But the stories set thirty years earlier in the narrating 'I's' childhood reveal that the 'old-time' Trinidad was already breaking up. The old pieties about nature are powerless to prevent the ruthless plunder of the forests; communal stability has already been uprooted by the pulls towards emigration, and any sense that Trinidad was ever edenic is undermined by images of the destructive power of alcohol and the casual presence of paedophilic sexual abuse.

Rahim's Trinidad, is though, as her final story makes clear, the creation of a writer who has chosen to stay, and she is highly conscious that her perspective is very different from those who have taken home away in a suitcase, or who visit once a year. Her Trinidad is 'not a world in my head like a fantasy', but the island that 'lives and moves in the bloodstream'. Her reflection on the nature of small island life is as fierce and perceptive as Jamaica Kincaid's *A Small Place*, but comes from and arrives at a quite opposite place.